PROCESSING THINGS

MICHAEL A. ARNOLD

www.darkmythpublications.com/

> The sale of this book without its cover is unauthorized. If you purchased this book without a cover, you should be aware that it was reported to the publisher as "unsold and destroyed." Neither the author nor the publisher has received payment for the sale of this "stripped book."

This book is a work of fiction. Names, characters, places, and incidents are products of the author's imagination or are used fictitiously. Any resemblance to actual events or locales or persons, living or dead, is entirely coincidental.

Dark Myth Publications, a division of
The JayZoMon/Dark Myth Company, LLC.
21050 Little Beaver Rd, Apple Valley, CA 92308

Copyright 2022 by Michael A. Arnold

All rights reserved, including the right to reproduce this book or portions thereof in any form whatsoever.
For information address, 21050 Little Beaver Rd, Apple Valley, Ca 92308

ISBN: 978-1-7372947-8-8

First Printing March 2022

Dark Myth Publications is a registered trademark of The JayZoMon/Dark Myth Company, LLC.

10 9 8 7 6 5 4 3 2 1

Table of Contents

Introduction..xi

PART ONE - AUTUMN

Country Boy Returns to University..........................01
Pylon..02
What Nubbed Treasure.......................................03
A Candle...04
Processing Things..05
Thought Fish...06
Delayed..07
Polonius' Dilemma..09
Ram Skull..10
Sleepless Drive..12
Going Conker Picking.......................................13
Big Coal Bag...15
Shopping City..17
A Found Picture..19
The Barn...21
Just Wealth..24
The Bonfire..25
The Singer...27

PART TWO - WINTER

Pass the Heartless Day.....................................31
Death of a Pit Pony..33
An Old Hall..34
Rain, Steam, and Speed.....................................35
Seals in the Sea...37
A Wedding Photograph.......................................38
Scraping Ice Off My Car....................................39
Birdsong...40
Terribly Cold..41

Table of Contents (Cont'd)

Christmas Tree...42
Snow Falls...43
A Bird Flew Alone..45
On the Lake Side...50
Driving Home..52
A Night...54

PART THREE - SPRING

Sunrise...57
Never On the Same Road Twice.......................................58
First Spring Mists..59
Afternoon Shoot..62
A Tree in the Road..64
The Petrol Station...65
Morning Dawns Over Florence..66
Crossing A Dead River...69
Stargazing(?)...71
Lotus Beer...73
Purgatory..75
    Part 1: Eyes Closed..75
    Part 2: Momento Domum Dei...................................83

PART FOUR - SUMMER

Mushrooms 95
A Memory of Australia...96
On A Bridge...97
Time Bird...98
I've Often Noticed... 99
Sitting in a Summer Field...100
Urban Pastoral..102
The Old Cottage Ruin...103
There Is No End To This...104

Table of Contents (Cont'd)

Masks	105
The Divers	106
Among Divinities	107
The Cedar Path	108
My Neighbor's Marlboros	110
Summer Schooling	111
To Be Born's A Sin	113
A Fox, Hunting	114
This Last of Meeting Places	115
Flooded Church	117
Trip To Kielder Water	119

PART FIVE - REFLECTIONS

Seasonal Haiku	125
Three Poems About My Grandfather	128
Beginnings	132
River Time	133
Protests	134
Seeing The Lindisfarne Gospels	135
The Ice Sea	136
Scyld	138
About the Poet	141

*For my friends and family
who mean more than they can know...*

Notes and Acknowledgments

Some of these poems first appeared, some in slightly different versions, in *The Furious Gazelle, Bard of the Isles* and *The World of Myth*.

'Noli timere' (p. 10) is reportedly the last words of the Irish poet Seamus Heaney. "What is the use of talking / when there's no end to talking?" (p. 24) is a slightly adapted quotation from 'The Exile's Letter', a translation of an old Chinese poem, and 'Dante will put this man in hell / because he's sabotaging peace' (also p. 24) is also a slightly adapted quotation of 'Sestina: Altaforte' - both by the American poet Ezra Pound. 'the dead's best shroud is a starless night' (p. 39) is a quotation from 'The Death and Life of a Saverino' by Elizabeth Bishop, taken from the centenary edition collection of her poems. 'Nil igitur mors est ad nos' (p. 59) is taken from the Leob Classical Library edition of Lucretius' *On the Nature of Things*. 'in principo creavit Deus caelum et terram' (p. 86) is taken from Genesis Chapter 1 verse 1 of the Vulgate Bible. 'Felix qui potuit rerum cognoscere causas.' (p. 102) is taken from the Penguin Classics edition of Virgil's *The Georgics: A Poem of the Land*.

Introduction

These poems were written over the course of a few years, in different periods of one person's life. Even so, together they tell of a single year in that period – trying to understand and process things that make the world feel confusing and somehow bigger and more connected than might have been realized in the past. Everyone probably knows something of those 'dark nights of the soul,' when there is some question in the back of your mind that will not settle down and let you sleep.

The modern world, full of 'distractions from distractions by distractions,' can be disorientating. There is often a wish for the quieter, more bucolic life of the countryside, but nature is never really as kind or peaceful as it might seem. There is a war in every woodland, a fight for survival in a world that we humans have cultivated to make things easier for us and for us alone. Even in a country like the one these poems live in, very much peopled and settled, you can see glimpses of the wild nature that is always just behind the surface – just under all the tarmac roads and expansive cities. The wilderness is always near, wherever you actually are, especially the wilderness in our own minds – just as there is a wilderness in the dark forests of information and impressions as we try to work out the nature of the universe around us. Not just how it works, but what it all means.

Poetry, by its nature, allows the reader to co-create the poem with the writer. When something is read, especially when it is descriptive and fictional, everyone will imagine something different in their heads, or will have some slightly different interpretation of what has been said. The image of a tree or a beach will be unique to the individual because our imaginations all work in different ways – as is the way we think. It is always surprising how many different interpretations of the same thing there can be. When that happens, can I really say an interpretation is wrong? I know what I think, but in one sense anything you read is not the writer's, is not anyone else's, it is yours and yours alone. What these following pages mean to you is going to be unique and can even change. That was certainly true writing them. More than one poem started life as one thing, and then it became something else when I returned to rewrite it. I had, between the first writing and the rewriting, changed as a person. I had lived, thought, and read a little more, and was able to come back with a slightly different perspective.

All of these poems mean something special to me, so I'm putting them out there. The first poem I ever had published is here, as is a very long and complicated and very personal poem that took two years to write and get it right. Going back over them and compiling them has been a strange experience honestly: you can remember exactly what made you write some poems, others just seem to come from some place in the unconscious and they demanded to come out and be heard, other poems you do not remember writing at all. Creativity is a weird and illogical form of magic I think, and in a strange way I am happy it is illogical. I think if we fully understood what creativity is, it might make it less special somehow. As such, I really want to thank everyone who read the early versions of these poems and gave feedback and encouragement over those years. Writers' first audiences will always be themselves. The second will probably be the people they trust. The last (if they are lucky) will be complete strangers. So, I also want to thank my publisher, David K Montoya, and my editor Stephanie J Bardy.

But I want to say my last thanks to you, the person reading this book. I really hope you enjoy it. There is a lot here: experiences, memories, doubts and hopes. Any first book is going to be quite a timid process, and I am not going to lie: this has been quite scary. But, in life, you have to be brave. So here we go …

Michael A. Arnold
February 5th, 2022

PROCESSING THINGS

PART ONE - AUTUMN

Country Boy Returns to University

The night stars, I'm going to miss them
light up the dark sky, like Dante's god.
From here, on this cold hill, it seems
the earth is dark, but heaven is bright.

I'll miss the stars when I go back
to late night, streetlight revelries,
and a heaven so polluted and orange
that the sky might seem empty to you.

To me they are two separate worlds:
cities of people and man-made stars,
the country with the lingering gods -
one poorly reflects the other.

Pylon

I wondered the edge
Of a desolate lake –
Soft ripples on rocks
Talked to me alone.
A white bird-trail line
Arched high overhead;
A rusted pylon stood
Against the ancient sky.
I had somehow forgot
We still needed them.

PROCESSING THINGS

What Nubbed Treasure

I once asked my old professor
"can you tell me what it was like,
meeting Seamus Heaney himself?"
She told me after a smile:

"He could step into any room,
and everyone would turn to look -
he had this aura, you could say,
solid and indefinable."

Years later, to honor the man
when I'd heard he'd died, I went to
a Viking-furrowed North Sea shore
with a copy of one of his books.

I only read the poem 'North'.
It blew back against the long, dead beach -
like sandy grit caught by the wind.
Then (in darkness) I turned back.

MICHAEL A. ARNOLD

A Candle

This could be a candle -
A small light in a dark place,
Like a cabin without power
Because of a storm.

Shivering like it's cold,
This light emits a long
Dark line -thin, shivering,
Rising into the blank air.

Processing Things

Scratching the crumpled
autumn ground,
working
        the rake,

my eye watches
as I work outside,
taking everything in.

MICHAEL A. ARNOLD

Thought Fish

Something about the surging sea,
Ocean deafened voices
Give white ideas –
Still fresh after passing:
Thought fish amusing themselves.

Delayed

If Dante were alive today
His version of the River Styx
Would be a train station pub.
The murmur of chatter,
Like it would still be there
With no one around to make it,
Is all that can be heard.
The room is a thick dark brown,
And a thick dark atmosphere
Hangs over all.

I am here,
At this table
With a beer,
Waiting on a burger.
Outside, a train is waiting,
Being seen to by many,
Making many sounds.
I reach for my bag,
Fumble for my train tickets
To check they are still there,

MICHAEL A. ARNOLD

And feel for my copy of *La Nausée*.
And the train outside just sits,
Waiting for something to happen.

Polonius' Dilemma

I heard the trailing west wind
sweeping through empty streets,
while little pools of rain muttered
like Orestes at his crucial moment
I decided I'd do it, I'd step out.

MICHAEL A. ARNOLD

Ram Skull
Noli timere...

It could have just been rock
sticking out mossy ground,
dully rain dark
and weatherworn.

Johnny took an interest,
and pulled at it.
It murmured something
around soggy peat,

Leaving an opened mouth.
glistening grass-shards
thrown up
with the movement.

I saw a cave,
and two moon craters,
cricket ball sized.
"A skull," I said.

PROCESSING THINGS

Already knowing all,
Johnny admired it;
sighing as he wiped
loose, black dirt -

A wet clump fell off
and slopped to the ground,
and for the first time ever
I was afraid.

MICHAEL A. ARNOLD

Sleepless Drive

A sleepless drive
through a hard rain:
falling brown leaves,
a thick blizzard of
autumnal fallout
(like snow)
Spread everywhere
around their trees

Like an overturned wine glass
over a clenched hand
the ink is not drying.
Poetry, I know,
is a discipline
lost in translation.
Here, only the blizzard remains.

PROCESSING THINGS

Going Conker Picking

Autumn nights can be very cold, you know.
Sometimes, they take me back to my childhood
When I would go conker picking with dad,
In the front of his old brown Ford Escort.
We used to go collecting them from the trees
Lining a long country road to Morpeth.
The fields flowed so fast past the window,
All the warm, cold colors of deep autumn.
The country was preparing itself for winter.
The man liked Bob Dylan, and 'Maggie's Farm'
Was playing louder than the car engine.
I remember dad said, "You are very quiet?"
I did not answer. Just shrugged my shoulders.
I was thinking of Derek Jacobi
Playing *Richard II* on TV.
"What's up?" he said. I hated that question.
"Nothing," I said, not wanting to answer.
I don't think anything was on my mind.
"You are quiet," he said, "seem deep in thought."
Nothing more was said, until "here'll be good."
And Dad pulled over, and doors clunked open.

MICHAEL A. ARNOLD

A northern wind crackled the treetops,
As fire-like leaves shuddered on their wicks,
And streams of light ran through the branches.
That was the purest air I ever smelled:
It was thick with the odor of wet wood
Like animage of lumber mills not quite there.
"Look along the edge of the road," dad said.
I did. Holding on to a stone farm wall,
I picked a conker out the grass. It was
Still inside its sea-mine-like rough shell,
I picked at it, trying not to spike myself,
Until it broke away – offering up
My prize. It looked like a little plum
With a coat of highly varnished wood.
I loved the way they looked and felt in my hand.
I saw another conker on the road,
A car had smashed it, sending a soft fluff
Of yellow inside rotting everywhere.
"Here's one," dad said, holding a plum-thing up.
Pocketing the one I found, I walked over.
Dad's conker was much bigger than mine.
I liked the way the veins showed its strength.
I took it and hugged him. We soon drove home,
I could feel the two conkers in my pocket.
Funny, I don't remember how they fared.
One could have been thrown away with that coat
And I would not be the wiser for it.

PROCESSING THINGS

Big Coal Bag

We were told, "if you don't believe in Him,
There'll be nothing for you in your Christmas
Stocking but a big bag of black coal."

There was something about the way the sound
 'Chingching, chingching!' would rumble through the
rooms
 When the old man worked at his anvil.
 You'd think it sounded like a clock chiming,
 Or something like the telephone ringing.

I once went into his workshop:
An anvil and grindstone in his garage.
The man loved to work and work metal,
He would sharpen neighbor's tools for free,
And once he sharpened one of our axes
So fine, I swear, it could have sliced a tree
in half with a single, powerful stroke.

He was being taken to live in a home
One day. He went quietly, with dignity.

MICHAEL A. ARNOLD

He did not look to see who was watching,
But he must have felt a hundred eyes on him.
Everyone mentioned how he was wearing
The iron crucifix he had made for his wife
The Christmas before she passed away.

We, being good neighbors, helped move his stuff,
And that is when I went into his workshop.
I played with the grindstone first of all.
Sitting at it, and peddling until
The wheel was spinning very quickly –
Like the wheel of a bike at full speed.
And then I tried the hard, cold anvil set.
I had always wondered how it worked,
And how he used to make the metal glow
Like he was working the stars of heaven

An observation made that mystery clear:
A small coal furnace in the corner,
The kind that's sold in a garden center
For heating an outside seating area.
I left wondering how many bags of coal
Had been feed into it during its life.

PROCESSING THINGS

Shopping City

We would only go into town
When we needed the shopping.

I remember seeing all the tall buildings,
and being curious what each one was.
I would always ask from my back seat.
By the time I was old enough to know,
I knew the police station,
the radio station
where the football is played,
the offices buildings,
the many storied car parks
with glittering stars
sparkling from cold streetlights.

And then we would go
to one of the supermarkets,
where you parked
and had to walk a mile
over tarmac covered with
smoked cigarettes

like brown autumn leaves
to the shop doors.

When we finished gathering,
I used to stack the shopping
onto the rolling service belts,
and make my own city.
First the heavies:
I would make boxed curry skyscrapers.
Then big sports stadiums of milk.
Lines of cleaning and washing fluids
would serve for government buildings.
Big shopping center stretches
of meats would come next.
Then tins –
the lower-class housing
bunched tightly together,
with the instant coffee
acting as little corner shops.
Then came the lazy bread suburbs,
with cup noodle packets and baby bells
that were parks and cafés
for the people to relax in.

My city was always dismantled,
filled into the trolley,
and we'd go home
to store it away.

PROCESSING THINGS

A Found Picture

In a box of childhood things,
I found a book of holiday
pictures. Looking through it, I found
this picture of baby me:

There's a young, man-like pose,
In an ill-orange lit taverna,
Wearing a Nirvana T-shirt
That is way too big for me -

Long, fat dangling spaghetti lines
Hang from a smiling, childish face,
Smiling with all the squalid joy
Of a life lived without purpose.

It is so strange to see this now.
Imagine a person's life as a stone,
On a rocky river shoreline
When the river can't push it more.

Many stacked stones make an era,

MICHAEL A. ARNOLD

Then being cut out the rocky earth,
Like from some hot Attica quarry,
And used to build a Parthenon.

That rock that built the Parthenon,
Must have come up from the earth.
There's just loose stones on the surface -
Deeper, the rock is more solid.

PROCESSING THINGS

The Barn

The cooler breeze did not move the trees.
A late orange sun had stretched overhead
So, the hedgerow paths seemed to be glowing,
Even the old barn did as we approached.
Matty pulled the broken lock out the door,
And let it thump on the gravel-mud ground,
Then we were in. The barn slowly found shape
From the darkness as our eyes adjusted.
The floor was flat dirty grey concrete.
Iron branches held up a rusting roof:
A big hole had been punched into the sky
That, at that hour, was not admitting light.
The once-sweet scent of hay still lingered there,
Haunting the place with ghost-like memories.
It was absolutely perfect for us.
After a mumble-muffle of bags set down
It was straight on to serious business:
Dan set down a tall dark bottle of rum
He had stolen from his dad's drinks cupboard,
The name on the side read 'Kraken Black Spiced'.
We sat around it, like around a campfire,

And took turns to drink straight from the bottle -
Matty grimaced with the force of the taste,
And Dan stuck out his tongue with a "PAH!"
Then Dan had some joke about Mat's sister
(We all liked her then) and everyone laughed.
That was the first time anyone had spoken.
The broken barn withstood some light breezes,
But its old iron walls moaned like zombies.
We settled down to talking about girls
As we passed the bottle of rum around,
Playfully mocking each other, as friends do.
Everyone had three drags, which was enough,
Before we got into our sleeping bags.
The glowing color outside had faded,
The wind-wolf started blowing the barn walls.
We kept talking until we fell asleep.
I do not know what woke me that night,
But the heavy shivering of cold dew
Ensured that I would be staying awake.
The moon was watching through the hole above,
And as I lay, looking at its scarred face
I saw a ghost-like owl high above us,
Sitting on the main roof beam like a king.
No idea why – my head turned slightly,
And it turned its head to look back at me
And it lurched forward, as if to move,
But stopped itself, thinking better of it,
Shifted again as if to tell me something,
And then it relaxed on its throne again,
Like we had invaded his small kingdom,
His empire and with iron scepter rule,
Regal in a lonely pandemonium,
Then there was a small sound, like a cat hunting,
He fell into a blackened corner of the barn

PROCESSING THINGS

And there was a squeaking squeal of pain,
An incandescent alarm, that soon stopped.
The owl appeared again from the shadows,
Flying up to sit back on his throne
And nibble away at the lumpy catch.
But then there was a squelchy, squalid thump
As the rat corpse slammed into the concrete,
And suddenly I was terrified.
The owl, thinking better of coming near us,
Flew out the hole in the rotting roof.
I sat up, for some reason, to hear more:
There had been something satisfying
In that pathetically soft, squalid thump
But I did not hear anything more.
There was nothing but the sound of winds,
Of the world around us quietly alive.
I was not the first to wake up next morning
When the sun's rosy fingers stretched from high,
Across the vaulted dome of the sky,
And straight through our barn, on a way to nowhere.
There were small spikes of grass growing inside
The barn, between the walls and the flooring
Shy in exploring their territory.
They vibrated in an unfelt wind rush,
And when everyone was awake we left,
Poking fun at each other, as friends do.
But something big had changed during the night.
I did not tell anyone about the owl,
But as we walked away from the barn
I remembered how it looked so lord-like,
And wondered what it must have thought
To see us sleeping in his hunting ground,
Which felt like a newly abandoned kingdom.

MICHAEL A. ARNOLD

Just Wealth

What is the use of talking
when there's no end to talking?
Dante will put this man in hell
because he's sabotaging peace.
But now he sits with the poet
and chatting like an old friend -
the golden sun dims in the room.

"If you are upright, Boniface,
you will be a friend to me."

PROCESSING THINGS

The Bonfire

The first bonfire I remember I was six.
The last, dead red leaves of autumn clung to
A comfortless, shockingly hard north wind;
But a bonfire had been built in the field
Behind the first school, and piled up so high
It would burn for most of the night.

In the somehow dead glow of the streetlights
The bonfire was the ghost of color.
It was a tall, weird hill of orange wood
Like something that had always been there,
And our village had been built around it.
For some reason, it kind of scared me,
And I vice-like squeezed my mother's hand
Which made my wool gloves squeak like Styrofoam.
I hated how that squeaking made me shiver.

When I heard a shucking, shucking, shuck
Of oil thrown on I heard everyone
Settle – trying to savor the moment.
The wood started to crackle and kindle.

MICHAEL A. ARNOLD

Soon the fire had spread all over it,
And people started throwing on more –
Anything flammable, and no longer wanted.
Teenagers started acting up, and danced around,
Shamanesque, and it was something to worship,
Spraying the bonfire with cans of spray
Causing explosions that lit up the night;
As if the bonfire was an angry god.
The people laughed, with blue cans of drink
And steaming mouth sticks. You could get so close,
Red flakes of flame would burn your cheek.
It was, I know, the warmest I have ever felt.

And so many bonfires that must have
Been burning across the country that night,
They must have looked amazing from the sky.
All the little dots of light in the night
Signifying that there is life down here.

The Singer

Coming to the pub stage
With an afro-haired guitar,
she struck a few good chords,
starting a newly weathered song.

First by some slick rock band,
here the fast-flowing melody
felt primal, somehow natural -
each syllable was a surprise hit.

With curly red hair beating
like the waves of sound
against the shore of the crowd,
her foot and pick kept time.

Then she started singing,
and the swelling rose and burst:
everyone in that pub sang along
like it was an old folk song.

PART TWO - WINTER

Pass the Heartless Day

The mud moans underfoot
all the way down. Old-stone lanes,
like mortar between bricks,
make up the strength of the land.
A plane moans high in the sky,
and distant cars can be heard -
modernity grumbles.

You cannot be sad among
the dead land of winter;
the hills and trees stand unworked,
Split by rivers cold enough
to snuggle ice shards. The
bubble-laden grass nods,
agreeing with the wind.

Everything seems so quiet
under the long grey sky.
There is a perfect reading place
under black column trees,
with so many branches

no hard rain could get through.

Small, shy birds look about for
any food to be picked.
The shivering sheep and cows
huddle close together;
they share some body warmth,
against the chilling rain.

PROCESSING THINGS

Death of a Pit Pony

The fog had rolled in thick that night
And the street looked like the rain.
A wet, sick light was coming in,
Matching the dining room's orange light.

A horse was lying on the table
Slowly in-taking gasps of air,
A rising, rising of dirty hair
Told everyone that Mabel,
The last of Ellington's pit ponies,
Was fading away from our life.

In her eye, an ill-weak light
Soon faded, like her breathing. Only
Her human friends were there beside her,
Who breathed short sighs, saying "aw."

Remembering the strength, she'd been before,
Each person still held love for her -
But there was little more to do now.

MICHAEL A. ARNOLD

An Old Hall

It looks like a field
of rain wet wheat,
standing vertical
against the sky.

Lines of furrowed
red brick suggest the
long and hard work
spent on the building.

Like it was loved
once, it stands proud
between dull graffiti,
and plastic office blobs.

This could have been
a haven of idle joy.
Are there happy ghosts
under its domed roof?

PROCESSING THINGS

Rain, Steam, and Speed

A drizzle of oil becomes heavy rain,
It covers the whole canvas land with a
Vague suggestion of living countryside.
It looks to me like a windswept moorland,
A place that is unfriendly to mankind,
Reacting against our drab use of it.
Is that a town there, to the left of us?
It does look like it, with a tall stone bridge
Just before us, bright despite the weather
Attacking for who knows how many years.
You can just see some buildings fogged out by
A moving, misting cloud of water drops.
That rainfall feels like it is drenching us,
The artist worked well to create that effect.
A boat on the river, rowing to shore,
Suggests the downpour came on quickly.

Those dabbing hammers of rain pummel earth,
As if nature wishes to rework man,
And this little piece of land has become
A kind of workshop for the blind forces

MICHAEL A. ARNOLD

Water is a part of. Yet, despite all this,
Here comes running towards us a beast:
It is sort of like a straight, black worm.
Its bellowing suggests it's great strength
As it races out of the murky fog,
In defiance of the angry landscape.
A flurry of misty rain is fleeing -
The iron monster does not care, it is
Screaming, and howling, and smoking thickly,
And as it does it builds up a great speed
Like it is trying some way of escaping
A land formed by nature and nurture.

PROCESSING THINGS

Seals in the Sea

The seals off the Seahouses coast,
Rough with rocky gull-song islands,
Swim-play around in the hard surf.
Their cat-like paws will cut downward,
Sending many white bubbles down.
Like how they will dive and dive for food,
Then rise to breathe in cold white air;
Then, again, they'd dive into deep jade
Cold water, a great dark fog bellow.
Amazing - life has grown so used
To living off that rocky coast.

MICHAEL A. ARNOLD

A Wedding Photograph

A small tree has been planted.
A couple stand together,
holding a shovel's clean trunk.
Lifting her hemlock dress end,
and tip-toe standing in mud,
aunt Penelope looks happy.

PROCESSING THINGS

Scraping Ice Off My Car

Each sweep made little diamonds of snow
which floated up into the streetlight's glow,
then drifted down, starring the dark road,
would stay a second, and then disappeared
like little dots of light with no gift for sight,
and the dead's best shroud is a starless night.

MICHAEL A. ARNOLD

Birdsong

He spies me as I come nearer, still singing.
Then, still eyeing me with raptorial suspicion,
He leaps, lifts his wings, and his singing stops.
I watch him fly up, lifting my spirit.
But I'm still happy with my feet on the ground

PROCESSING THINGS

Terribly Cold

Lighting fires
every morning
with the papers
of yesteryear –

getting glimpses
of happier headlines
being consumed
in inky smoke.

MICHAEL A. ARNOLD

Christmas Tree

A damp, snowless Christmas day:
Spears of presents sit waiting,
Like the pikes of wasted wood
Holding up the low lunar sky,
Like an apocalypse delayed.

All the build-up to this day is
The greeting of the green knight
Who welcomed us into the woods
Where we as children ran about
Looking for those little toy stars.

PROCESSING THINGS

Snow Falls...

on the black road,
which seems to absorb it
as it cascades down,
as cars storm angrily
both ways.

So many flakes
fall that grey morning.
Each one is as unique
as it is barely noticed -
quickly melting.

Seeming detached,
the movements of cars,
each looking different
going somewhere slightly
different.

In the long city gloom
of the coming rigid night,
that always seems to come

MICHaeL A. ARnOLD

at the best and worst times,
the ice will start to form.

PROCESSING THINGS

A Bird Flew Alone

A bird flew alone
over the village on a
cold and snowy day.

A young artist sat
with a worn-out sketchbook,
watching the bird fly.

It flew overhead -
over the snowy graveyard
the artist sat in.

She had hard shaded
the gravestones a stark black,
to contrast the snow.

The bird landed on
a branch on a nearby tree
and eyed the artist.

The tree looked somber

against the brittle snow.
It drooped as if sad.

The wind breathed a sigh.
Creswell church looked quite gothic
In the joyless day.

Both sat – existing -
for a moment neither moved,
then the artist said:

"A bird, huh? Funny -
if I had your wings, I'd fly
somewhere better."

Unable to talk,
the artist translated the
look in the bird's eye.

"And where would you go?
The whole land is white like this ...
what are you drawing?"

The artist smiled
at her own joke, pretending
that the bird could talk.

"I don't get humans:
being a bird is lonely
yet you want to fly."

"Yes – I want to fly -
I want to see what you see

PROCESSING THINGS

up there in the sky.

I imagine that
just being able to fly
is so liberating.

Seeing everything
holding on to earth below
must look beautiful.

I would love to fly.
imagine the inspiration
from feeling so free."

"That's the funny thing,
I return to the same places,
even though I fly."

"If you can tell me,
what does the white land look like
from high in the air?"

"I can tell you, yes,
there is a strong connection
between us, human.

It looks dangerous.
A frozen, animal woodland
talking wildly.

Ice-dusted houses
humans do not share with us,
but share them with cats.

You shoo us away,
but look after wounded birds
like they are children.

But we are no better.
Birds disrespect what they have -
want things they do not."

"What is it birds want?"
"We want to understand things
the way we see them."

"How do I know that?"
The artist asked herself as
she looked at the bird.

"I told you, human,
there is a connection now
between our two minds.

It is not often
that we get to converse
with our souls like this.

Must say, I like how-"
the sound of a motorbike
scared the bird away.

Watching the bird climb
the artist felt somehow sad,
something had been lost.

Mind full of flying,
she returned to her sketchbook

PROCESSING THINGS

thinking of the bird

She thought over what
the bird had told her about
a life spent flying.

Turning a new page
she imagined what it saw.
and began to draw.

It was her village
seen like a bird would see it,
she liked what she drew.

She had no idea
if she had talked to that bird,
or what it would think

if she had showed it
a drawing imagined from
its own perspective.

MICHAEL A. ARNOLD

On the Lake Side

Pale winter morning - passionately cold.
The lakeside runners came out from the trees
As the frost reigned there, a total control

Of the whole area with a snow-freeze
Fog. Watching the run from my open car,
Not sure I'd run on a morning like this,

I liked the way the low sunlight there
Danced on the lake surface. My friend was running,
And while looking for her, on clean, sharp air

Floated the sound of some quiet talking.
There was something harsh in the tone, I thought,
Knowing I was listening, the wind was stinging

Hard against my face. What little I caught
Was something to do with someone cheating -
But they must have moved on because I got

No more. That really got me thinking:

PROCESSING THINGS

How common are betrayals? Then the cold
Air woke me, my friend's run was finishing.

MICHAEL A. ARNOLD

Driving Home

White snow is spraying the road
from one snowbank to the other -
10 mph – headlights stream
a boreen path through the night.

Car warmth is too comfortable.
The lifeless air should be keeping
me awake, but I can feel
the skin around my eyes closing.

Stopping in the gateway of an
endlessly white farmer's field,
looking like a warm bed duvet,
I felt myself falling asleep;

And the stillness in the car
was like the stillness in the air.
With my breaths fast-gathering,
I sunk into the driver's seat.

Starting to decline into sleep,

PROCESSING THINGS

turning my little red car off -
only hearing winter howling.
Car warmth is too comfortable.

MICHAEL A. ARNOLD

A Night

It was a dark, stark winter night,
snow had stopped growing the ground,
and all things shone with a moonlike light,
and nothing living making a sound.
There was just a slowly tolling bell –
stuck twelve times, then died as well.

A snoring from an earth worn-out
(an old man under a duvet)
which got me thinking about
a thought that I had had that day:
what makes me want to live,
other than being alive?

PART THREE - SPRING

Sunrise

I had never seen
A calmer intensity.
From a bleak horizon
An atomic inferno
Rose with red passion,
Shone on the world,
And lit up my drive
To work.

MICHAEL A. ARNOLD

Never On the Same Road Twice

Trees in the dark, lit up by my headlights,
Shine as I drive through the grizzled midnight.
They all look like trapped souls of the damned
In a disturbed and living agony.

As I pass, I look into their faces
Twisted and gnarled with thin motivation.
These things have worked all their adult lives
To bare leaves that will go in their season.

Of course, there is an order to all this.
As the hour changes, symbols change too:
To live is to change, to change is to live,
As such tangled, dead thickets have before.

PROCESSING THINGS

First Spring Mists

"Nil igitur mors est ad nos"
And so, death is nothing to us.
Lucretius

I.

Are the first mists of spring
the winter frosts leaving?

Driving to work
early one morning.
The white cotton fog
was a thin quilt
stretched over the earth,
and every tree
a small iron nail
to keep it all down.

II.

Mouse feet rainwater
against my car roof.
I shut off the
radio to hear it.
Cloud water spraying
from the cars in front,
makes a fog of gloomy blue.

It is as if
these cars are ghosts
moving peacefully on

III.

The fresh world smell
after a spring rain
is clearing out old ghosts.

All the dead leaves
from the last autumn
are now scattered
with new grass rising,
wet with rainwater -
one generation is
sacrificed for the next.

IV

Stopping for a drink after work.

Feeling the solid wood
of my old table

PROCESSING THINGS

by tapping it
ritualistically,
reading funny memes
on my phone.

Light rain hits the window.
As the log fireplace cackles,
someone at the bar is laughing.

V

I heard once
'By the earth's songs
in the colder days,
you'll find your way'.

But a boy's will
is the wind's will -
and it is easy
to not remember
to pay attention.

VI

The mists are gone now.

My main beams are strong
but they can't see everything,
and I don't mind that.

Driving through the dark
is always calming.
You can almost feel
the coming winter
almost a year away.

MICHAEL A. ARNOLD

Afternoon Shoot

Two gun-bangs came from Fairwinds House.
The shadows of turbine blades drifted on
uncaring, like the leafless trees between
long fields making the roads look damp.

Then quiet, with late winter warmth,
and soft mushy cracklings in the hedges.
Then there was a cool click crick clacking
echoing from the grand stone house.

Through all the rich, ornate rooms
(thick with roasted chicken and pigeon)
coffee, carbon, and conversation came
drifting through the open windows

Gyre talk, about if they'd 'got one',
and if they had ever hit the real thing.
A few sly smiles as the gun was lifted.
A pull. A frumpy throw. Then: bang.

"I think I missed the bloody thing"

PROCESSING THINGS

as the heavy iron beast bowed its head.
"Don't worry about it, son," was said back,
"life gives nothing without hard work."

MICHAEL A. ARNOLD

A Tree in the Road

The storm rain hit last night,
it had been pretty bad -
it split a tree, which fell
onto the dust-grey road.

I slow my car to halt
and check the satnav map.
It's funny. I could have
sorted this out with an axe.

But I don't have an axe.
No one does these days.
All I do is turn around
to find another way.

The Petrol Station

From out the downy forest,
A many branched γραμμα,
He pulled into the petrol station

Beside the dull computer tower
Of the Ashington Sports Centre
To complete an automated task.

MICHAEL A. ARNOLD

Morning Dawns Over Florence

A morning rose
across the city,
and the ringing,
ringing church bells
told believers to be
Mass–bound.

Like every morning,
I would get up from
my cheap hotel room,
and grab the bus
to the center
of Florence –
to soak it all in
before I went home.

I must have spent hours
dodging the bikes and cars
flowing through the branching
thicket of narrow streets
that Dante knew.

PROCESSING THINGS

Watching people
trickle into the room
of The Birth of Venus
and Spring by Botticelli
in the Uffizi gallery,
and eating the ice cream
with the violet sugar
in the rooftop cafe,
that cost about 10 euros,
which I couldn't exactly afford
but was totally worth it.

In la Santa Maria del Fiore
watching believer's bend
to light the candles
on two stands
with hundreds of arms,
like two small trees
with fiery,
autumnal leaves.
Then looking up,
through heat-mist,
at the inside of Il Duomo,
the blossoming paint
pointing to the light
of the heaven outside.

Then finally watching
from Ponte Vecchio
the sun dip down
to the land below it.
I will never forget
the dying, wine–red sky

MICHAEL A. ARNOLD

reflected in the surface
of the calm river water.

Yes, all those memories
flowering up inside me –
that was a kind of pilgrimage.
But why can't I write about it?

PROCESSING THINGS

Crossing A Dead River

I crossed a dead river –
With a young spring
Burning behind
The river grove.

Out of all this beauty
Something must come,
But the times are as serrated,
As the long claws on trees,

Like a newborn lamb
Coming out its mother
To flop in the grass
Never to move

We all write
Our own epitaphs
Into the sands
Of the world.

There is a form

MICHAEL A. ARNOLD

Of formless meaning
That is felt
And not defined.

All interpretations
Order words
Into language,
Like a grammar,

A structure that is
Always being tested
By a nature that takes no side,
And feels no pity.

The hills breathe
A long slow sigh
Flowing everywhere,
But not saying words.

PROCESSING THINGS

Stargazing(?)

It's something to do
whenever abroad,
see all the different stars
in the watery sky.

Are they the same
tiny spots of light
we are so used to
seeing up there?

Science tells us
they all died long ago,
but they are still there,
and still powerful.

Before the great light
bursts into the sky,
they were what
ancient sailors went by.

Picture it: wine dark

MICHAEL A. ARNOLD

whale-roads, wood stemming,
as sailors look to heaven
for guidance,

like those Phoenicians,
or that Greek who
made history
in planetary wanderings.

Time means nothing to stars
already dead.
I like to think
they are teasing us:

another land
on the horizon,
another idea
of great adventure,

They, in life and death
keep life in death.
Err - but how many
are manmade?

How many rocks
are on this shore?
How many are sirens?
How many suitors
are waiting for us,
daggers in hand?X

PROCESSING THINGS

Lotus Beer

"Here – I bought you a pint mate, what's up?
You look like ya got somethin' on your mind.
W-why do you not speak anymore – speak!"

"What do you want to know?"

"What's on yer mind!"

"Err. Well, I've been – been thinking about things."

"Johnny, what is it on yer mind, mate-y?"

"Well – you know one person can't know it all?
like, even the smartest fellas go'en
they don't know everything there is to know."

"No."
  "No?"

"That's right, they can't – how could they?
Like that proper bright lad, we went to school with

MICHAEL A. ARNOLD

(I don't know why you're jealous of that guy),
smart guys like that spend their whole lives in books,
and do not have the foggiest idea at all
what half the words in those books even mean.
And don't know how to talk to guys like us."

"It really makes you wonder, doesn't it?
if there's any point at all to anything.
people use words not knowing what they mean -
people have lives not knowing what they mean."

"The problem with you is you think too much.
Sure, we are thick as dog-shite, but you know,
some things are not meant to be thought about."

"They are not meant to be thought about?"

"Life's too short and hard to make it harder -
why not just drink up, mate, enjoy yourself?"

PROCESSING THINGS

Purgatory

Part 1: EYES CLOSED

1

There I was,
behaving as wind behaves
through long grass.

With my door open,
my feet on the hot road,
I was sitting, smoking -

The cooling heat smell
on ivory-colored dunes
mixed with my cigarette -

Summer was
dripping down
the sky.

MICHAEL A. ARNOLD

A swirl of sand
blew over the road
and into the open car -

The Portable Dante
in the passenger's seat
seemed to talk.

But music killed the silence -
the Porcupine Tree CD
Deadwing was playing,

but it died when
I cut the engine,
walked onto the beach,

and was alone
with the waves, winds
and whisky sky.

Watching the sea
I lit another cigarette,
knowing it was bad for me.

The sinking sun
peering from the water
lit a long, golden path -

one I could not walk.
I was happy enough to go
my own way, along the beach

and through
a dark forest of thoughts

PROCESSING THINGS

so wild, savage, stubborn.

I remembered her sitting there
on the sand dunes beside me,
eyes closed - feeling it all.

Running sweat,
like it was sunlight
flowing out of us,

I stopped at a small stream
running into the sea,
and turned back.

When my engine revived,
so did the car and the radio -
and music killed the silence.

Have you ever stopped
the car during a drive,
when you're alone,

thinking that from here on
your life beings, and all you've known
had been a series of lessons?

I remember thinking like that
in that night-dimmed services station,
when we came back from Cornwall.

I remember sipping coffee
in the cool consumer lights
illuminating all the vanities,

MICHAEL A. ARNOLD

as the steam of small dots
on the distant highway moved on.
There's no philosophy without misery.

2

On the edge of the water
I reached my sanctuary,
after strong gusts of wind
blown me, lustily, about:
a familiar lakeside pub.
It was a comfortable place,
tools and piles of firewood
and black and white photos
making it feel nicely bucolic.
I, feeling like the dead,
bought myself a black coffee
with the few spare coins, I had
and sat beside the window
with my book of Dante,
marked at canto eight.

Looking at the cloudy lake
under a colorless sky
what thoughts I had disappeared –
like dead leaves falling from trees.

Then a book of memories
flipped open in my head.

The first thing that came back:
camping in woods with friends,
as teenagers often do.
Alcohol bottles all around

PROCESSING THINGS

as we worshipped our campfire,
feed with the twigs and branches
we snapped and torn off the trees.
I remember being so drunk,
looking at the dead moon
through a thicket of branches.
Heavy metal music blared
from our brick-like phones.
I remember falling over
going to relieve myself
of the beer I was drinking.
The dirt path faded away
when I fell on the wet grass,
trying not to get my phone wet.
"Oh god," I laughed, "oh god."
My friends had to use the light
from their phone screens
to find me in the darkness.

The memory faded away
and something else came back -

A round hut of mossy rock
in a thick, red leafed forest.
That dun temple of moss was
the end of our pilgrimage.
The info board outside it said
inside you would be able
to hear the sounds of the sea,
like putting a conch shell
right up against your ear.
Inside, shutting the frigid door,
the autumnal light vanished,
our chatter quickly trailed off.

MICHAEL A. ARNOLD

Then we could hear it all -
I was by sound transported
to a large room, with a glass wall
looking out on a rough sea –
the room bare, cold, unlit
against the grey winter out there.
The surging ocean slammed,
white rage, against the rocks.
When the moment was over
we crossed back into the world.
Outside we stood on the shore
of a glittering amber lake.
Walking back to my car,
the wood brown road squelching,
our walking Facebook selfies
were posted for all too see.

Then a cold and bright May morning.
The cherry blossom falling
onto a dirty city street
like snow from the iron sky.
Water had pooled in the potholes.
I walked into town alone,
soul aching with emptiness,
looking for a place I could
exist for a little while
without being disturbed.
A bookshop, I guessed –
a castle full of knowledge.
How many times must
that have happened?

PROCESSING THINGS

3

Then a voice inside my head
broke the echoes

I was parked on a long road,
darkened by dead porcupine trees
hanging in the ghostly mist overhead,

listening to the wind
and the idle clicking of my zippo.

It said 'all poems are fragments'.

Then someone was
at the driver's door,
in a thick winter coat
with the collar up,
bare headed
hard mouthed,
like an old Greek philosopher,
knocking on the glass.

And I was out,
face to face with him.

He said, "I know you,"
and called me by my name,
"what are you doing here?"

"Nothing."

"Nothing? What do you mean
nothing?"

MICHAEL A. ARNOLD

"Nothing."

"And that's the problem,
isn't it?
Everything flows around you,
yet..."

I looked away in panic,
and the words
in hoc signo
came to mind,
and then a pause.

I looked back.
He had vanished.
I thought I knew him
as the shade of
someone who had died
years before.

Wood groaned -
mechanical-rain pattering
from high overhead,
the trees bothered
by the wind
moving on.

That had set off
an inferno
in my head,
melting that lake of ice.
I was then in my car,
speeding through
dead and dying leaves,
an idea of where to go.

PROCESSING THINGS

Part 2: MOMENTO DOMUM DEI

1

It was raining.
That kind of
ghost-like,
mist thin rain
you walk through
without feeling.

Gray day,
no shade anywhere.
Lindisfarne village
felt lifeless.

But damp clung
onto everything.

The quiet breathed.

Mature houses stood either side.
A little further down the way
the old, rain-worn cobble streets
of the village stopped abruptly
on long fields of blustered grass,
that, to my eye, looked endless.
I slipped into a small pub.

It was warmer inside. A TV
was going through the news,
with monochrome pictures
framing the wall around it:

MICHAEL A. ARNOLD

fishermen smiling beside
rope piles and ship ribbing.
A nice place for people to be

But it was empty.

The barman was
the only person
I properly talked to
all day.

I got a room,
the other side of the village
from the monastery ruin.

Down the road
from the main church,

I walked up a thin
sheep shitty hill track,
with dark rock sticking out
like broken bone.

I pulled myself up
to look down
at the stones
of Lindisfarne monastery.

It looked like a giant's
death-frozen hand,
reaching up
to the sky
with cobweb-colored fingers.

PROCESSING THINGS

There was something in it -
not beautiful
but meaningful.

I wanted to know a way in.

That night
a damp darkness
shrouded everything,
a kind of cool fog
draped over the world.

The few iron tree
streetlights stood
against a smooth
stone wall,
shining bad light
onto them.
I don't know why
but that was comforting.

I was walking
to the church.
A dewy wind came,
and I breathed it in.

In the darkness
the ecclesiastical walls
looked haunted
by the night -
but the arch
over the door
still pointed to
an impossible

path above.

I could hear the sea
slamming the rock
of the nearby shore.

2

There I was,
my back to the mural wall,
hearing someone speak
from many years away.
'in principo creavit Deus
caelum et terram'
came rippling out from
a figure of red
on a pulpit.

Dry light coned in
from the open door
gave new energy,
and I ran out
into the bright,
damp morning
outside.

The church was before me
the monastery ruin behind.

The room was stale with nostalgia.
Cluttered with old furnishings -
an egg shaped glass on the wall
reflecting the darkness.

PROCESSING THINGS

I lay awake in bed,
struggling to sleep.
I could see,
in my mind's eye,
a tall, grim faced priest
the mirror could not see
looking at me
through a wall of time,
and he talked to me:

-who are you

-a pilgrim I think

-and you
what are you doing here,
one who has never believed

I could not respond.

-poems are like prayers,
a private communication
with the world.

-I guess

-why do you not believe

-it's logical

-there are many things logical
that are not right

-I guess

MICHAEL A. ARNOLD

-you have to be brave.

-but I'm scared

And then there was a release,
like a door opening
in the small hours
onto a snowy field.

Walking around Holy Island
trying to understand the world.
With the moaning wind
blowing the dew
from the uncultured
hair of the world,

and as I walked
the sea-watching coast
I was haunted
by the indefinable
wrongness with
the world.

And by the lives
I could have lived.

Memories
are ghosts
of the
ever present
past.

But they fed something

PROCESSING THINGS

foaming inside,
I guess everything did:
'We are unhappy people
in a happy world'
it might have said.

And time
seems to slip past
and vanish
before you notice
it happening.

When I reached the causeway
it was starting to flood.
The sky was clear,
and the life-giving sun
was settling
into the water.
I watched
it sink away
as I walked back
to the village.

As we get older
the world gets stranger.

3

The path to heaven will begin in hell,
wasn't that the point of Dante's journey?
Real understanding is always hard won,
and it might never actually come.
Thinking about this as I wake the last day,
ate something, drank coffee, and chatted

with the owner of my inn for a while.
She was old, and carried herself with ease,
like the moon's face in the morning sky,
and she said she liked living, even though
things had not been all that kind to her.
She said she thought that "living is suffering,
but that suffering – pain - is good – in a way,
the way our bodies tell us something's wrong."
I mentioned why I'd come to Holy Island
she said, "it's best not to think too much, though,
I don't know much about a life after death,
But you've got to have a life before it."
And she gave me a warm, dry smile.
Talking is our small way of admitting
we are all alone here, together.

With the day rising, I checked out of
my room and went back to the car.
At the causeway I did not look back.

A boat, a boat, a boat, a boat, a boat -
all along the rotting waterfront, rocking
together while at rest. The sun was high,
I'd grabbed a coke, and was sitting there
watching the rolls of the water moving.
The slosh, sloshing lapping against the stone
Pier, awaking me to a new mindset.
What is wanting cannot be numbered
for the person always asking questions,
but it does not matter what you think,
because faith is not a logical process
it is something that comes into all things
in one way or another. Or is that right?
I don't know – but I have not seen

PROCESSING THINGS

everything out there, in the great unending.
Increaseth knowledge, increaseth sorrow.
And when you are trying to find yourself
you might accidentally miss yourself,
since you're lost in a sea of information.
because while you might know certain things
you might not really *know* them properly.
You can know something without knowing it,
and you can know something without knowing.
The same thing can mean different things
at different times. The monarch of the sky
Burst out from a line of stubborn clouds
and the seagulls on the drenched waterfront
sang rejoicing in his glorious honor.

Looking out to sea, the world is out there,
beyond the misted horizon, where time moves.
I think I was wrong about Dante.
while his journey does start in Hell,
his purgatory is on the world, here,
while above all of us is a universe.
We try to live by what we think is true,
which is a kind of private tragedy
because this is a world of suffering.

The sun is the right star for wisdom,
it helps all travelers see their paths
and know the roads they are walking,
and as I went back to my car
I thought I heard a gull call after me
"Go, go, go!"

PART FOUR - SUMMER

Mushrooms

White stools grow in patches like fur,
they seem to like the damp places
and clump themselves tight together,
where the best chances for life is.

An early warning of autumn
through trees: the great fireball's shine
spreading on the moss skyscrapers,
a great red - the day's in decline.

MICHAEL A. ARNOLD

A Memory of Australia

On the foreshore
Having a drink
In a Dome cafe

A spark
Dancing
Shimmers
Electrically
On the water
Surface

Last life
Dying
Sunset
Warm red
Falls

PROCESSING THINGS

On A Bridge

Over a river that goes
out to sea, swiftly flowing
through that stagnating summer.
Look - that small island down there
where we used to play as kids,
overgrown with trees and fern -
our dream of an unknown world.
I'd like to be there again,
playing all those old games,
letting the world disappear.

MICHAEL A. ARNOLD

Time Bird

At closing time, I heard the cry
"Drink lads, time's getting on!"
It made me sigh an upset sigh
Because I wanted to drink on.

At the wet dark lake, to drink on
In the bird watching shed,
We drank and joked until dawn -
Using the seats like beds.

What, seeing the dark dome of night,
Throws that great stone high,
That burns such a purifying light
It makes all the stars fly?

Because of it, the hermit hours
Glowed red as I walked home,
Bird songs and rising flowers
Followed my steps' metronome.

PROCESSING THINGS

I've Often Noticed...

I've often noticed people changing
In weather, when it starts raining.

People look angry at their phones
While happy shop music drones;

Something must happen to the brain,
A smile seems harder to maintain,

And on the roads, people forget
The basic rules of etiquette.

Like the drooping branches of some tree,
We don't like it when the weathers shitty.

MICHAEL A. ARNOLD

Sitting in a Summer Field

By a field of grass (like flapping paper),
sat under a tree - trying to get lost
in my battered copy of Robert Frost's
complete poetry. I think much clearer
out in the untamed sounds of nature.

I know the sounds of the winds very well,
and now there has been a change in the air.
Coat over book, in case of rainwater
from a new dark smudge in the wet sky art -
I know dabbing rain is about to start.

I climb the tree to get a better look
at the coming Charybdis in the sky,
giving everything in a wet, dark dye;
looking like it will have soon overtook
where I've been sitting with my book.

Frost painted his landscape in perfect,
I think, art - as a 'some kind' reflection
of the world, based just on his perceptions -

PROCESSING THINGS

there is nothing true in any of it.
Until a second eye agrees to it.

MICHAEL A. ARNOLD

Urban Pastoral

Felix qui potuit rerum cognoscere causas.
Virgil

I saw, in a game, rain falling on tired bins.
It looked sad, congested, by the glum building
That rose up beside them. It had me captured,
Not quite in the way long fields of green wheat
Waving like the surface of a peaceful lake would.
In a video game - what cheers me more
Than finding such fine detail in a world?
And I don't know if such things mean anything -
Or how many people would just run past it.
Or is this just a Barthes myth confused?

The Old Cottage Ruin

There is a rotting cottage that I know
Must have been abandoned years ago.
It's far from the village, like a hermit,
And I do not know who owned it.
Now all that's left is the stone and wood
Frame, greenery growing where it could
Get any sunlight. No ghost of life there -
And it was once a home. Who will care
when it has disappeared?

MICHAEL A. ARNOLD

There Is No End To This

Jacques the philosopher
on the moon-like beach,
raving theories about
"that atheist Lucretius,"

moves out,
toward heaven
and the distant
night-lights
in the sky.

Clouds of foam
slap against him
before dissolving,
forcing him back.

"There is no end to this!"
he shouts back at
our hotel's bar.

Masks

Acting: a costume to wear
To put on different airs,
Covered in the jewelry
Of ancient mythologies.
Aiming for different goals,
All actors play their roles.

I'm always playing in tragedies,
But tonight, the play's Aristophanes.
I am too used to tragedy's airs -
This is a mask I shouldn't wear.

MICHAEL A. ARNOLD

The Divers

They dive from rocks,
Stone beaks curved like a bow,
Cracked and sun-hammered by time.
They shout open vowels as they fall,
Some kind of primal language,
Into the olive green water.

Among Divinities

Above a quiet harbor,
Tangled olive sticks
And crickets are singing

As we are eating seafood
In a quaint taverna,
Watching a fisherman.

He is humming a tune
As he brings his day's catch in,
An image from *The Odyssey*.

And we enjoy our meal
Imagining ancient legends,
Out of place and time.

Shining among divinities,
The sea-god seems to rest
Under the cooling sunset rose.

MICHAEL A. ARNOLD

The Cedar Path

'Beauty is truth, truth beauty' – John Keats

The terrible heat
around the Halkidiki
olive trees' frames
coated the dirt road
of the cedar path.

The well-healed air
of the Mediterranean
filled every atom.
I was drunk on Mythos,
my heartbeat to it.

Perhaps it was the heat,
the trees had cracked
dark lines across them,
like light shadows
of crinkled faces.

PROCESSING THINGS

It was beautiful
with imperfections.
If beauty creates emotion,
is there beauty in ugliness,
and so, a kind of truth?

Those trees stand
against the hard sky;
a shield of leaves,
not covering the ground
as I walked on.

MICHAEL A. ARNOLD

My Neighbor's Marlboros

You'd smoke a Marlboro every morning.
Silent, breathy gunshots while sat in bed.
Then cough and cough before getting ready.

Then you, who once fought in North Africa,
Would troop down to your old allotment,
To spear at weeds and set new rhubarb seeds.
When in the mood, you'd have another smoke,
To clear your lungs. Once you gave me a ten
To run to the shop and buy a new pack.
I can still hear the hacking, rasping sound
I heard then when I walked away from you.

PROCESSING THINGS

Summer Schooling

Fun was all we had to live for, it seemed -
Not a single worry, but our Hobbit's den,
Out in the kid-rumoredly haunted dene.
Running there; the dinted, grainy farm lanes
Went past the petrified ends of the mine,
A scholastic alter to the curse of life,
The red God of our village. In that summer
Heat we were totally free. Flax color
Pools tried to stop us, fly-clouds covering
Every slop-step, until trees closed on us.
The hairy green earth become a wood-spike floor.

We'd built our den around a coal black car
Covered with some kind of sticky red tar -
In that dene, we'd sit and break flowers
By the side of a the thin dene river
Until the air of a garden center
(Cold peat, fresh soil, mold, and ripe heather)
Filled our fat nostrils, and our hands would be
Thick-coated with dirt. Then the silent trees
Would watch us throw rocks at our ruined car,

Without judgment. But I would think
Our den was ours to rule as we saw fit.
It was our land, and we cultivated it –
Lording over our little twig kingdom
Like we were living a video game,
Building a new world. Those summer days
Were great fun.
              When my best friend come saying
Our den had been washed out by the rains
The night before, we ran those old farm lanes,
And across the ill-looking swamp one last time
To see it all. The dene wood was autumnally
Dead, the river had broke bank, came our way
And washed our little dene-country away.
The wood and coal shards we had collected
Had disappeared – and the burnt car shell
Was just a grimy scrap of metal plate
On the surface of the hard-working stream.
That was the last time we went back there,
We had lost control of our tiny world.

To Be Born's A Sin

Depression is a rusting water tower.
Both are a hollow soul
and a hollow brain
stuffed full of water,
and the corruption of filth
slowly killing the once strong structure.

MICHAEL A. ARNOLD

A Fox, Hunting

The haunter of ferns and long-leaf woodlands
goes on a food-hunt, close to the village,
and silently walks up to the chicken field,
leaving a line of prints in the cold earth.
he stops – there's a wire mesh obstacle.
Still hiding from the light of the bright sun,
he spies on the clucking creatures stirring
as they beat and peal away at the earth,
not knowing he is hungrily watching.
The wire-mesh fence stretched before his eyes -
he cannot get at them, so he moves on.
But as he does so, he can't help look back -
like someone, having struggled out at sea
but now safe on shore, looks back in fear.
After he moves on the farmer will find
his prints and try to work out what they mean.

PROCESSING THINGS

This Last of Meeting Places

Parking in a cliff top car park, long beach
Waves were hitting the cold, white-gray sand.
I turned my back on the untalking land
And went down a weak, craggily grass path
Soundtracked by an angry seagull's laugh.
The balding sand dunes looked just like a wall
That stood many years ago, and its fall
Spread rocks everywhere to catch the sea-sand
Drifting in, spreading more beach on the land.
Smells of sea and seaweed were on the air,
Either side of where I was standing. There
I stood for a while, watching the short life
Of wave-water rubbing on the shoreline
Like waves of a living conversation heard
Blurrily through a wall. Again, laughs a bird -
White-tailed Eagles often came to these shores,
But they don't cross the North Sea anymore,
It's sad, their time and culture has passed on,
And any that were native here are gone.
I then imagined someone in Norway
Looking out to sea, and looking my way,

MICHAEL A. ARNOLD

On a beach that looked exactly like mine
And, like me, thinking things to pass the time.
I felt a strange connection was established
For a weird moment, then it vanished,
As has happened with people I have met.

PROCESSING THINGS

Flooded Church

A smell of rot
was thick on the air.
Through hopelessly
squeaking grass,

the lake sweats oil and life,
so, it is hard to look
into that green,
the oldest known green,

and see the foundations
of the church - like an attic
full of forgotten, dusty,
raven-haunted boxes.

Memories and thoughts
cannot find land,
to carry the dead
from that lifeless place.

But the roof and steeple rise

MICHAEL A. ARNOLD

from the sickly water,
arched like an arrow
toward heaven -

the sky thick
dun and still,
against the world,
hung over everything.

It would be hard
to get in there now.
No boat will take you
from the shore.

PROCESSING THINGS

Trip To Kielder Water

1

When we went in, the resonating stone
Cut off all sound. That glum temple of moss
Would be the end of our cool pilgrimage.

The information sign outside had said
You'd be able to hear the sea in there,
Like putting your ear to a big conch shell.

Huddling inside, we shut the frigid door
Shutting out all of the wet brown wood light.
Our fleecy chatter trailed off to silence.

I was by sound transported to the surge
Of storming water slamming my head's shore.
Breath beads caught, and for a moment died.

Nature stopped moving to indulge itself,
I could feel him standing there beside me.
When the moment was over, we crossed back

Into the world, feeling clean in the shades.
Then the afternoon allowed itself breath,
We stood on the shore of a huge, glowing lake.

2

We went back to my car. The brown wood road
Was squelching - in protest of our walking
Facebook selfies, with trees in the backgrounds.

Music flowing from my phone to one ear,
The other headphone dangled, was swaying
Like a long thin branch waving from out a tree.

Crossing a dead bridge, littered pine needles
Completed the rich air. You let it fill you,
Like walking past fresh doughnuts at market.

The oldest of us walked on fast ahead.
The shallow furrows across her face were
Grass wires on the bank of a still river.

She said: "Hey, do you know the way home?" "No,"
I said, "I'm very sure my satnav does though.
I don't think I could live without technology."

3

That whole trip was not an escape, for me.
'Escape' is when you don't want to come back
Very different from a distracted retreat.

How can you really escape from the world?

PROCESSING THINGS

Each journey like ours' to Kielder Water,
Makes us see another part of the earth;

Which can be uneven. In Dante, all the
Souls in purgatory ask the pilgrim,
Again and again, for prayers to help them

Get to heaven quicker. While all the souls
Trapped in Hell ask only to be remembered -
At least in Hell we'd face consequences.

PART FIVE - REFLECTIONS

Seasonal Haiku

Autumn

1

Speaking truthfully -
The light fall spiking through trees
Is so beautiful.

2

Hard rain slams against
A pile of discolored leaves
Causing it to talk.

Winter

1

Ducks by the lakeside,
Looking at the cold water.

MICHAEL A. ARNOLD

They look sad, somehow.

2

Snowdrifts lap the town
As people return from work
In the fields, singing.

3

Snow clouds run across
The wide, empty field of white.
A lifeless vision.

Spring

1

The thick fogs of spring
Are pressing down on the world -
Image of autumn.

2

Is all this sunshine
Warmth from the coming summer?
Time changes the world.

PROCESSING THINGS

3

Warmth radiating
Through the grim office window.
Outside, birds sing free.

Summer

1

Night out. Uttered drunk,
True feelings turn into lies
The morning after.

2

He chases his ball
Straight into the flowerbed:
Dog at barbeque.

3

Riverside drinking -
Time rushes on pleasantly
In this man-made world.

Autumn again

1

Fog smothers the world,
Obscuring many dark trees.
They almost snarl back.

MICHAEL A. ARNOLD

Three Poems About My Grandfather

Sergeant Patrick Arnold – Durham Light Infantry 1934 - 1943

I - Being Back Home

Being back home was nice, but strange.
He could not tell her what he had done:
The commanding officer had denied
His request to leave base, see his first child.
So, he just walked off, and all the way home,
Along long, unsympathetic roads, north,
To be with his newborn family.

The baby was sleeping in the mother's arms,
They talked about the future. But it was not long
Before the police came to get him, and he
Left for war, wanting to say so much more.

PROCESSING THINGS

II - Night before Capuzzo

Like those soldiers in Homer,
The night before the battle
Was spent lying under the
Innumerable eyes of God,
More real than ever before –
Somehow. Not all were nervous.

They'd be off in the morning.
Bearing the ammo packs,
The gruff-cordite of small arms
That will growl in the attack,
Like two bears fighting for a prize.

III - Battle at Fort Capuzzo

1

Against the wind
that whipped along the surf.
and a heavy weight pushing him to earth.
He reached the wall
as rifles cracked,
and blistering machinegun fire
crackled all around.
It did not make him
go to ground.

Part of General Wavell's Desert Army,
in the compass attack,
he had ran at Fort Capuzzo
like a demon sick of sin.
No cannons, no tanks.

MICHAEL A. ARNOLD

Just short-range gunfire.

A flash of helmet.
He looked over -
the heaviest fighting was on the airfield,
Bodies were scattered
like dead leaves,

The sun blasted down on the hard,
dead world.

A wave of shrapnel,
his wall was peppered with bullets
And he went down hard.

Then German tanks were trundling past.

Dragging himself into a sangar,
almost acting dead,
the battle went on
not noticing he was down.

2

The stretcher-bearers came,
there are some fifteen
or more
severely wounded comrades.
He guessed the lad across from him was bad,
and he could do nothing to help him.

The next thing he remembers
was wakening the next morning,
the lad lying across from him

PROCESSING THINGS

was dead.

The Germans said
any man who could not sit up
would be left
to the desert.

Knowing what that meant,
he had to struggle to pretend
he was better than he was.
But it was hard,
So hard.

Then,
imagining the yellow
flower of the broom,
that grows wide and bright
in the endless moors of home,
that spurt many flowers,
and come back each year.
That plant is said
to be a sign of plenty,
and to tame the wild -
and who knows
if that is true.

Thinking all that,
he forced himself,
heaving,
Herculean task,
to sit up
and live.

MICHAEL A. ARNOLD

Beginnings

Everything is better when just begun:
The first bite of a meal is the most pleasant,
The first mile of a walk, you feel so much better
The first glass of beer on a hot summer night,
The first idea of battle, first moments of war –
It is always right to fear the endings.

River Time

I think, now, that time is like a river flow,
burbling and bubbling as it goes -
smashing and jumping on craggily rocks
meaning the great events of history.
As I think this, the river still streams on,
What if God himself stepped over this river,
as he was moving on to parts unknown?
It cannot speak, so cannot tell the facts,
(never miss a chance to not say a thing),
and we are left guessing at what we hear
in whispers that sound like speech. Some say
our life is one long struggle in some dark
rain beaten cave, all hoping for fire.
While other caves nearby may as well be
the craters on the surface of the moon
flowing in orbit around our planet.

MICHAEL A. ARNOLD

Protests

A large crowd of the young,
And they are all freezing
In spite and anger,
Screaming at horses,
Who do not understand
Their sounds are words,
Meant to communicate.

PROCESSING THINGS

Seeing The Lindisfarne Gospels

"Don't touch the leaves," our teacher said
"they'll be dirty" as we were being walked
to Ashington's Woodhorn pit museum,
    To see the Lindisfarne Gospels.

In a non-pretending, large room
Full of bone house treasures from days long gone,
And pictures of monks, and Vikings in ships,
    We were guided toward the book.

    You could feel the age of it.
It looked like a thick block of bone dirty gold,
Trapping so many crumpled autumn leaves
Inside a history-old word hoard.

    I was not interested then. But,
Looking back, the book made the past real –
An artefact not undivorced from our own
    That we will, somehow, leave behind.

MICHAEL A. ARNOLD

The Ice Sea

Hammered North Sea beach:
The gloomy, rusted blade
Of a longsword.
Under a sheet of brittle ice.

This ghost-loaded sea
Sometimes spits up
The blackened shells
Of old bones -

It saw an age of
Ice and iron,
Forging the bones
With crackling mead fires,

But this water
Is just one part
Of a much larger,
Much richer whole,

It was here,

PROCESSING THINGS

Two cultures clashed:
The sunburnt Iliad
And the rain-drenched Edda -

The always moving
dialectical bridge
of stone-like history,
that shapes us all.

But I don't think
This ice sea
Can be condensed,
Or be contained

Like this.

PROCESSING THINGS

Scyld

After Beowulf lines 1 – 53

What do we know of the Spear-Danes,   in the old days,
when the ruling kings   had real strength and glory,
and these hero-prince's   heroic and honorable victories.
Often Scyld-Sheafing,   was the scourge of armed men
from many nations,   and seizer of mead halls.
He was a terror of the troops,   even from the time he was first
found a foundling, destitute at sea   (a humbling experience for him!)
and aging under an honor-cloud   he prospered well.
Soon, the surrounding peoples   sharing the sea,
that great whale-road,   had to yield to Scyld
and pay him tribute.   That was one good king.
Soon a boy-bairn was   born to Scyld, and he became
a good young man at court.   It was said the good God sent him
as a comfort to the Danes,   knowing what they had tholed;
the threats they overcame   without thane or lord,
and for so long a time.   Then the Lord of Life,
that glorious ruler,   gave a child as a gift to the world;

MICHAEL A. ARNOLD

Beow was the boy's name   and his fame branched out
as Scyld's son,   until it spread across the north.
So it is: a young man   must accomplish good deeds
under his father's protection,   and give magnificent gifts,
so, in old age, his friends   will stay standing with him
when war comes.   So it is in all nations:
only by praiseworthy deeds   does a man prosper.
Scyld was still commanding   when his destined time come
and he travelled over   into The Lord's protection.
His dearest comrades   carried his corpse
to the surging sea currents   as he himself had asked,
his word was still law   among the Scyld-Danes
as befitting a loved leader   who had ruled for so long.
Down in the harbor was   the ice-ringed prow
of a prince-fit vessel   ready for the seas.
They laid down the king   they dearly loved,
the great ring-giver,   in the heart of that ship
famous by the mast;   and there was much treasure
from distant parts,   much gold brought with him.
Never have I heard   of a vessel so stuffed
with beautiful war-dresses   and weapons of battle,
the swords and mail-coats   were laid on his chest
with heaps of finery,   that, with him, must
depart, and drift far   into the ocean's flood.
No lesser gifts   could they have gave him,
the treasure of a people,   than those who,
in the beginning,   set him adrift
swaying over waves   to be no one's son.
Having a gold standard   placed over his head
his people set him out   with heaving hearts
and minds full of mourning.   No man knows:
no man of the hall   nor warrior can tell
who, in the end, it was   who found that vessel.

About the Author

Michael A. Arnold is a graduate of the University of Sunderland and Northumbria University. He is based in North East England, and has previously published essays and short fiction. His influences include Seamus Heaney and Robert Frost.

www.ingramcontent.com/pod-product-compliance
Lightning Source LLC
Chambersburg PA
CBHW071508040426
42444CB00008B/1546